Jhalak Soti

Sustainable Eco-tourism in Pokhara

A Survey on Sustainable Eco-tourism Planning and Management in Pokhara Region, Nepal

VDM Verlag Dr. Müller

Impressum/Imprint (nur für Deutschland/ only for Germany)
Bibliografische Information der Deutschen Nationalbibliothek: Die Deutsche Nationalbibliothek verzeichnet diese Publikation in der Deutschen Nationalbibliografie; detaillierte bibliografische Daten sind im Internet über http://dnb.d-nb.de abrufbar.
Alle in diesem Buch genannten Marken und Produktnamen unterliegen warenzeichen-, marken- oder patentrechtlichem Schutz bzw. sind Warenzeichen oder eingetragene Warenzeichen der jeweiligen Inhaber. Die Wiedergabe von Marken, Produktnamen, Gebrauchsnamen, Handelsnamen, Warenbezeichnungen u.s.w. in diesem Werk berechtigt auch ohne besondere Kennzeichnung nicht zu der Annahme, dass solche Namen im Sinne der Warenzeichen- und Markenschutzgesetzgebung als frei zu betrachten wären und daher von jedermann benutzt werden dürften.

Coverbild: www.ingimage.com

Verlag: VDM Verlag Dr. Müller GmbH & Co. KG
Dudweiler Landstr. 99, 66123 Saarbrücken, Deutschland
Telefon +49 681 9100-698, Telefax +49 681 9100-988
Email: info@vdm-verlag.de

Herstellung in Deutschland:
Schaltungsdienst Lange o.H.G., Berlin
Books on Demand GmbH, Norderstedt
Reha GmbH, Saarbrücken
Amazon Distribution GmbH, Leipzig
ISBN: 978-3-639-32985-8

Imprint (only for USA, GB)
Bibliographic information published by the Deutsche Nationalbibliothek: The Deutsche Nationalbibliothek lists this publication in the Deutsche Nationalbibliografie; detailed bibliographic data are available in the Internet at http://dnb.d-nb.de.
Any brand names and product names mentioned in this book are subject to trademark, brand or patent protection and are trademarks or registered trademarks of their respective holders. The use of brand names, product names, common names, trade names, product descriptions etc. even without a particular marking in this works is in no way to be construed to mean that such names may be regarded as unrestricted in respect of trademark and brand protection legislation and could thus be used by anyone.

Cover image: www.ingimage.com

Publisher: VDM Verlag Dr. Müller GmbH & Co. KG
Dudweiler Landstr. 99, 66123 Saarbrücken, Germany
Phone +49 681 9100-698, Fax +49 681 9100-988
Email: info@vdm-publishing.com

Printed in the U.S.A.
Printed in the U.K. by (see last page)
ISBN: 978-3-639-32985-8

Sustainable Ecotourism in Pokhara

A Survey
On
Sustainable Ecotourism Planning and management
In
Pokhara Region,
Nepal

2011

Written By
Jhalak M. Soti
Ishaneshwor VDC -9, Lamjung Nepal,
Currently in USA.

(This Research Monograph is developed by re-writing the Masters thesis, submitted to Human Ecology, VUB, and Belgium at 2002.)

Acknowledgement

Heartily thanks to Andor Sperling, Acquisition Editor, VDM Publishing House Ltd, by providing an encouragement to write this monograph.

I especially indebted to my wife Priyambada Soti, for her felicitous remarks to my time, thanks for her. I respect with an appreciation to Mr. Balaram Parajuli for his cooperation and help during my field study. Thanks for offering photos Mr. Ram Mani Poudel. I appreciate to the photo selection helper Mr. Bikal, Mr. Bishwos Parajuli, and deeply love to my two kids: Subada and Suyog, who provided an encouragement and help during my writing. Finally, I would like to thanks to all my best wishers, relatives, and friends who were helped me directly or indirectly to my work.

Table of contents

Chapter I
Introduction

A developing poor country like Nepal has been recognizing as a traveling space world wide. A dominated concept of sustainable planning in Ecotourism has an aim to support the conservation of natural resources by protecting the right of local people to upgrade their economy. Pokhara region has a developing opportunity in Ecotourism since the history. Today, the locals are struggling to get the better opportunities against many challenges of the environment. A possibility to get the success of implementation has many factors. A concept of the description has the following data.

1.1 A background of Tourism

The world history of tourism has been recognizing since many years. According to Honey (1999), the first tour guidebook "Aimeri de Picaud" advocates the concept of the word "tourism". He has stated that the book was written by a French monk in 1130 AD, and had introduced some identical concepts of tourism as the religious pilgrims of that time. In addition, the book explores an objective of the visit applied for scientific investigation, geographic exploration, cultural and anthropological study of the world.

There might be many more tours in the history worldwide. The historical journey of Gautam Buddha has an importance in south Asia as a pilgrim. In an ancient history of Nepal stated that Buddha first visited Tibet as a religious pilgrim to advocate the ideology of Buddhism in the world. The century of Buddhism has been defining to the (563-483) BC and Buddha was burn in Kapilvastu of Nepal, offered his ideology of Buddhism from the Gayaa and transferred his massage by traveling in all parts of the north and the East Asia.

An historical concept of tourism found in Hinduism stated that in a beginning of fourth Century the first Shankaracharya (500 AD) traveled Tibet from India through Nepal. The purpose of his visit was defined to get a support of the people in Hinduism of that region and provided them to a guidance of morality principles for a peace.

In recent days, the tourism development is worldwide extended and the individual as well as a team mountaineering expedition has been increasing as a business. Developed countries are always in trigger of forefront among the others, while the developing countries are still in beginning steps to open the opportunities of the new possibilities. Nepal is one of the mountainous country belonging to the high Himalayas, mountains, hills, forests, lakes, plain and valleys explores a value for huge possibilities of Ecotourism development in the world. The history of tourism in Nepal has been found developing since 1950s. The country has been opened its borders to the foreign visitors since 1951 with a consciousness of democracy after Rana regime, and than the adventure and success of Tenzing Norgey Sherpa and Edmund Hillary were scaled the Mt. Everest (8848 m) at 1953. It made Nepal as a famous country to open the tourism opportunities in the world.

In the tourism history of Nepal, Pokhara is a best tourists' destination since 1969 after when the airlines connected through the capital (Katmandu) to the western sides of the country. In addition, after the construction of Prithvi Highway in 1976, the business has been uplifted more progressively in tourism of Pokhara region. As the beauty of nature, Pokhara valley has been supported by gorgeous natural lakes, deep river-cannons, forest ecology of the mountains, and a high Himalayan range towards the north. Fishtail, and Dhabalagiri peaks attract the center of Himalayas and highlighted to the natural beauties of the mountains.

Natural Beauty in Pokhara.

Regionally, Pokhara has the recognition of a historical Bazaar to the local farmers and traditional businessman. People from east to west and south to north have a motivation that the Pokhara has a history of importance in the business and in travel sectors. As a tradition since the history, a number of religious pilgrims had been trans-passing Muktinath through Pokhara valley by trekking and crossing the mountains' trails and the valleys from various parts of Lamjung, Gorkhas, and Tanahu and sangjha districts. Muktinath temple is a famous religious place for many Nepalese especially for worshiping and praying after while taking the shower of 108 taps of Muktinath. Such a religiously believer of the travels have been made mostly in Dashain festivals. It is celebrated two times in a year either on the beginning of summer or in winter, as the historical trends of Hindu tradition of Nepal. Many religious pilgrims have been visiting Muktinath in Dashain from other parts of the country and also from India.

Moktinath temple belongs in a great location across the central Himalayan territories in the western region of Nepal. Here, the climate is dry and windy and the land has more similarities with Tibetan Plato than the territories of Pokhara region. Everyday, twelve o'clock noon is forceful torrent generating time as the schedule of earth's Coriolis Effect on the higher Plato at the Muktinath area. Depending on season, the power of Coriolis Effect is varied, which can impact the visitors and pilgrims during the visit.

Muktinath area has wonderful geographical characteristics of the ground to excavate the artistic stones or rocks recognized as a symbol of god (Shalikgram) in Hinduism. Some experts believe that the artistic excavated fossils on the stones and rocks were supposed to made from marine fossils. The excavated location found above on 10,000 feet height of the mountain is believed billions of years old. The artistic stones with the ancient fossils have been used by Hindu pilgrims since the history.

In recent days, Muktinath area has been recognizing as an important visiting place for travelers. It has a tremendous value of nature to the religious as well as trekking purposes. It has also an importance to study an evolution of marine fossils or to the creatures of prehistoric times. Some local businessmen collect the fossil- printed stones and sale in the curio Shops and on the streets of lakeside Pokhara.

Muktinath is also a beautiful traveling place to the air travelers, and Pokhara is an important trekking route as a tress pass through either to go or at returning time to the tourists.

In the city of Pokhara, the second religiously famous place to visitors is Baraaha temple which is built in a small island of Phewa Lake. Baraaha is a name of goddess, logically important for peace prayers and naturalists who like the swimming and roaming with the nature of lake water during the visits. It also provides pleasure to the bird watching scientists and to other zoologists. Baraaha is also a famous place for religious pilgrims and visitors who enter to Pokhara city. The city has few other famous temples, for example, Vindabashini, Sitala, Bhadrakali, and Kalika and so on.

A phenomenon of attraction on Buddha Gumpa is another important visiting place to the foreign intruders and Buddhists. Buddha is respected as an ideology of peace in Nepalese communities.

Religiously, culturally, and historically, Pokhara is a city of harmony among the people of diversified communities such as Hindu, Muslims, and Christians and all are living in a harmony of simple life within the same society. Beyond the religion, the cast system is another important element in Hindu cultures. Nepal is a country of many religions and castes. Within the history of Hindu-based religion, there are four major castes and 36 sub castes culturally.

The cast system in the history has been continuing on the base of profession and characteristics of the family activities in daily life. The upper level casts and lower level casts were categorized by many points such as religious activities, dresses, tradition of foods and its types, behaviors and the richness of the family-tradition, etcetera. The latest development in the constitution has been made that any barrier due to the reason of casts is illegal and everybody has equal right of opportunity in the societies. Since the tradition, the last name of people generally characterized by the type of caste and the castes are defined according to the characteristics of the profession what they were doing since the generation to generation in the history of social development. As the affecting caste factor, cross-marriage relationship is also a key factor to move in lower caste to the groom generation and a few cases the bride caste move in one step upper level if the groom is from upper caste. An origination of castes is an interesting topic to the socio-scientists and finding to similar hereditary pool of the gene between caste to caste could be valuable to the genetic study for human history, and it also could be an important sample to the genetic scientists. Pokhara region is an example of diversified caste system in Nepal.

Pokhara region is magnified in an adventure of journey to the tourists. It has many aspects as an attraction of the aim of destination to many visitors. An opportunity to enjoy with new geographical architecture with natural assets such as the Himalayas, Lakes, forests, and the adventure of trekking are valuable resources to attract the visitors. In addition, a rural housing pattern and the model of traditional houses signalize a reflection of traditional human civilization of the history. Locally and internationally it has a high scope of trekking and a strong possibility to raise the future of tourism through a small productive investment plan without disturbing the direction of ecological sustainability of that region.

If we move forwards to implement the Ecotourism sustainability planning to manage in Pokhara region, it could bring huge differences in local liveliness to growing economy, business, and a standard. As the result, the development could further support to enter into a new era, by generating fund for conservation, developing infrastructures for facilitating the higher adventure and getting support to make a strong political empowerment of the community in that region.

1.2   Endanger beauty and challenges

A developing poor country like Nepal has been recognizing as a traveling space world wide. The adventurous mountains and Himalayas are recognizing with the highest peak of the world the Mt Everest, and the most beautiful inner Himalayan zone of Annapurna Ranges, the greatness of natural trekking fields, and some isolated geographical landmass provides an extra opportunity to the tourism market.

Pokhara is the western central mountainous valley of Nepal, which is recognizing as one of the important tourist destinations belonging at 200 km west of Katmandu, the capital of Nepal. The attraction of Pokhara is decorated with the endangered beauty of Annapurna Himalayan ranges associated with some environmental assets such as the lakes, forests, streams, hills and a greenery of mountains with a decoration of traditional human settlement as the villages.

A view from South-west, in Pokhara valley.

Literally, the word "Pokhara" defines a place for grazing land to animals with a safe area to survive in a group.

According to a local theme, the ancient Pokhara basically found concentrated in many small residential areas belonging with the separation of different sub-location (wards) by names and location. In a wide sense, today, the real meaning of the Pokhara defines the name of the valley which informally covers the surrounding villages, the flat plane landmass including the residential city, streams, lakes and hillsides. The main city of Pokhara is crowded, over populated and surprisingly polluted, while the mountainous vicinities are with low population and usually clusters in settlement, and are more closure to the ecological environment. The city areas are associating with big business centers, roads, vehicles, and with crowded population. While the villages are open with more fresh air and with no big business, mostly poor peoples' communities living same place since generation to generation as an ethnic group. Usually, many villages have no facilities of electricity, Internets, phones, and roads. But recently, many villages have been setting few facilities by making something better day by days. The opportunity in education, business, job, and transportation are really in poor level on comparison of the city, while the city is more crowded, more polluted and environmentally worse than the villages. The city life is expensive, over crowded, and in high risk of economy and in life than the villages.

Today, the concerned city pollution problem has been recognizing as an environmental degradation. The reasons of worsening situation might be the major causes such as a un-control open food market, unacceptable draining of domestic pollution, massive street shops, and over growing population and sheltering encroachment on the public properties, and so on.

As the practices to mitigate the problems of the city area, there have been some private activities in the past. According a resource of tourism office (2002) in Pokhara, few local organizations have been willingly involved time to time, as a volunteering job to improve phewa lake pollution and proving awareness in neighboring communities to control unacceptable pollution activities of the city but it has not stepping up in any necessary level except a slogan of awareness in practical. Few other community activities in local level also were started to clean up the city pollution in the past, but it was an increment and neither remained durable to back up into a clean city nor as a natural lake of the clean water. To upgrade the tourism environment, it is essential to manage the pollution problems of the city and lakes.

The attraction trekking is also associated with the tradition and culture of the remote lifestyles of the locals who have been surviving in a different world and in society with the comparison of third countries' environment.

In agriculture, many people of mountains and hillsides mostly use mix farming system that means people grow every thing by the same family and also in the same lands whatever they needed necessary to use in whole year and also keep cattle together in a domestic way. Mainly, the cattle define the cows, buffalos, goats, sheep, and pigs. Chicken farming is also more popular and domesticated in many cast and communities. Mostly, dogs and cats are used as common pets in the communities and many of them share as an out door survived without any ownership on them. These are more wild, hasty, and unattractive sometimes. Few people might have a domesticated dog and/or cats, which could be more trained and used to protect their house from stealers, and crops or grains from monkeys and mice.

The attraction to the foreigners by the cultures and traditions of the locals; some of the festival and cultures are specific pace to place according to the type of community, religion and caste. For example, a Gurung community of one location celebrates a type of culture and festivals that are not similar with Newar caste or with many other castes. The diversity of the culture is varied with the caste and communities. Pokhara region has a history of diversified culture with the castes, communities, and the religion. Now a day, the local cultural activities are devaluating and unknowingly collapsing through the incoming domination of the Hindi songs and further marketeering as an indirect encroachment of Indian culture in the society. The value of the Nepalese culture has been loosing its' power, because an unawareness to do safe relation with neighboring cultures, and has an unsafe interaction of the individuals and by responsibility takers in Nepal.

It is a subject of dignity to respect each Individual culture and an indirect challenge to the authority that to protect each national ethnical values of their own people.

Here in the tradition, many of the Nepalese people believe the guest as the god and the visitors are characterized as the guests. In very recent times, the meaning of the god is used as the feeling of the culture as the respect and a value, but it would not worked as an ancient Nepali tradition like free foods and free facilities because the world is dominated by the business in modern days. In reality, whenever you need a help to get out from the trouble, a morality of Nepalese culture could open the heart as the tradition, and help to save the life.

Sight seeing of Pokhara valley from the South- east

A trekking in Nepalese mountains could be a major part of enjoyment to the foreigners. During trekking, the visitors need guidance, information, better shelter, safe camping sites, personal safety, and other facilities to enjoy on adventurous living styles. Normally, the remote villages will not have better facilities as the need of the tourists. The hilly remote areas have no roads for transportation, and no enough residential infrastructures for housing and fulfilling the needs of luxurious life. In addition, there are many inadequacies in facilities such as in local communications, lodging and foods, qualities and quantities, and safeties during the time of trekking themselves. However, many villagers have a willingness to help and share moral respects among each others among the guests.

In most of the hilly areas, there is no availability of hotels, lodges or restaurants necessary to support for developing tourism. Even if they have, they might not sufficient to provide enough rooms and to fulfill the other needs and quality in management.

Many places of the mountains are remotes and hard to get in extreme in the depth of nature because there is no accessible way to found an organized destiny to view directly. An enjoyment of the trekking in an isolated geographical land is not only a difficult game but getting success in the trekking is another part of life. In such a visit of remote trekking can provide a combined opportunity to observe an extreme view of nature and an adventure of the leisure times.

Normally the mountainous trekking is difficult and the trekking routes are congested, and over-folded with the chances of misdirected to succeed the journey of certain destination. It should be managed with a real trekking path by planning to observe rare ecological environment by making accessible to the destiny without any natural damage or loss. Than after many tourists could get a chance to observe an adventurous of the nature and a life in mountain ecosystem.

In a current evaluation of the carrying capacity regarding the ecological vegetation and residential settlement, many of the mountains are virgin except some local interruption during the use of daily needs. Normally, the interrupted areas have no any re-plantation, selective plantation or not any organization of natural assets. The composition of ecosystem in many locations has been staying historically and not any manmade progress in the mountains.

The negative factors to impact the natural life of the mountains usually begins from human exploitation (especially deforestation) in the pristine forest ecosystem by forest firing and resulted erosion, and support mass sliding by summer rain, etcetera. The long term resulting effect can impact to the climatic change in the continent and in globe. In addition, high step flooding streams from mountainous territories are other problems to destroy the ecological habitat of hilly region. Every year, a million tons of soil and forest products flooded from Nepalese mountains to the Bangladeshi coast and an impact of flood destroys the crops and villages in Bangladesh (UNDP Report 2000).

There are no any major records as problems in soil-compaction in forest environment by trekking in mountains but few records of the unaware situation regarding destruction of vegetation by firewood users for heating and cooking purposes in trekking and camping fields.

The socio- cultural impacts of the tourism on local environment is another factor to evaluate the changes. People have no awareness about the loss of culture from different activities of the tourists. There is no training and education to the local people about how they can get maximum benefit from tourism industry and how to involve in developing Eco-tourism for a future of sustainability. Tourist education is also important part of this problem. The local authorities and government sectors are almost symbolic and non directive to move in many cases. The tourism education is not effective either in tourists or in targeted locals. There is no any necessary step taking by authority to develop cultures as an education. In education sectors, the activities are lacking, and laws and orders to protect the cultural value and ecological assets are not publicized or not ready made in authorities. An another thing for tourism education is uniformity in place to place for proper guidance about how to remain un-touch to observe local culture, tradition, and skills through an educative activity during the use of tourist facilities. The majority diversified ethnic people of Pokhara region is innocent about a plan or policy that to participate in tourism education in the past. It is essential to develop and use cultural exhibition in an educative and organized planning.

The another major impact of fragile political situation of Nepal has been bringing instability time to time to develop the tourism activities in the past two decades. As a tradition since 1995, the government has been unpredictably changing in a transitional time of democracy after displacement of the Panchayat monarchy and replacing new laws and order under constitutional King. In this situation an un-experienced new ruler could not handle perfectly to many problems and an unsatisfied reactionary group of political fringes might enforced the King to take revenge against democracy while some other unsatisfied communists specially the Maoists' had already started arm conflicts to displace political empowerment of multiparty democracy, Kingship and so on

14

an attraction of fishtail Himalayas, an adventure of trekking to Dhabalagiri among the Annapurna ranges. The high Himalayan trekking routes are not yet demarcated to the access for adventure trekking but some local trekking guides are more efficient to success guiding for scale to the peaks. If, it could be managed to the access of trekking and facilitate the camping sites in a managed scheme, it will make a huge attraction to the visitors for trekking and spent money in that areas.

The developing concept of Ecological tourism in a sustainable manner has an attraction to the future of tourism development.
Pokhara valley is the centre gate to the travelers who comes to visit the western region of the country. It is an important place for tourist destination after the capital Kathmandu and most of the tourists visit central Himalayan zone through the Pokhara valley and following the eco-track of Annapurna conservation areas. The surrounding Annapurna Conservation area project has a main objective for ecological conservation and to improve local development under the guidance of conservation principles of local natural resources and the public life. The conservation is important to promote tourism but not necessarily developed for over interference of that region. As the support of this objective Dr Horka (1990) approved a written massage in his book "Environmental management of mountain tourism of Nepal" as the specialist in the field of Geography. Additionally, this study deals with the pattern of tourism activities, its impacts, and carrying capacities of the natural areas.

Now a days, the ecological tourism is an important prospective of tourism development in the capital of nature. It is an application of the combining ideas of nature conservation and development in the areas of tourism which can maintain the beauty of nature and can support in the finance of local people. The conservation principle has a power to provide a solution to the upcoming problem of tourists' environment of Pokhara region, Nepal. It is necessary to improve business quality, tourism capacity, Environmental quality, and others supporting factors of the society. The principle of Sustainability provides equilibrium between natural environment and human society in a long run. Similarly, the prospective of sustainability in Pokhara region needs a further supports and a scheme of a new planning for further development. It is necessary to organize an ecological management with a planning of tourism development schemes.

1.4 <u>Study Objectives</u>:

The main target of the study has to focus on an Environmental improvement through a judgment of recent activities in the societies that has been affected to the human life and the natural environment. The study scheme of tourism development of pokhara region has been approved by collecting existing information provided by tourism industries, societies, and by other supporting factors of the environment. The scheme was developed by studying, analyzing and collecting appropriate guidance for sustainable Ecotourism as a new management scheme in Pokhara region.

The scheme of research objectives were divided into following categories:
a) Data gathering by using different parameters; such as literatures, news, reports, experiences, and field studies.
b) To indicate, and explore the important assets useful for ecotourism, sites, view points and trekking routes.
c) To collect public supports to the development of sustainability of Ecological tourism through a proper planning and a management plan.
d) To explore the possibilities of mutual benefits among the natural and the human lives through a development of Ecotourism scheme.
e) To point out the facilitating factors and key recommendations to developing sustainable ecotourism in that region.

1.5 <u>Results on Proposed Hypothesis</u>:

a) A new sustainable planning and management in Ecological tourism could be more appropriate than the present.
b) The mountains, forests, streams and lakes can raise the greatest potentiality if managed them in an approach of sustainable development.

The test of hypothesis were measured through the survey, including studied references and on the base of observation of the important natural assets that to find out a determination of sustainable development in respective region.

To test the hypothesis a quick response was collected during the time of focus group meeting among the participants of the different sampling spots. The question was "do you think the current tourism system in pokhara can provide ecotourism sustainability in the future?" The table below provides the participants' responses as the followings:

Table 1: Participant Responses towards the question as followings:

Sampling Areas	No. of participants	Positive response	Negative response	No. Answer
Lakeside	9	0	7	2
Talchock	6	0	4	2
Lakeside	5	0	4	1
Kalika	9	1	5	3
Kaun hill	6	2	2	2
Sundaridanda	5	0	5	0
Naudanda	5	2	1	2
Total	45	5	28	12

A Sample of field survey, February 2002.

The highest proportion of the participants was provided negative responses as the answer and they expressed that the current management is not effective to keep the clean environment in the city, streams, or lakes. There is an over exploitation in the lakes, Roads, city and streams due to mismanaging domestic wastes, encroaching the public properties for sheltering immigrants and by traditionally misusing social norms of gender right. That means the chances of sustainability in current tourism system is lacking if the planning and management is completely not improved.

In a similar test of the second hypothesis applied to the lakes, where as the overwhelming number of participants (33 out of 34) were supported the notion of natural assets. which was resulted such as the lakes can have a great potential if we can clean the aquatic vegetation, manage the human made wastes, and stop the over siltation in lakes.
The IUCN (1997) has approved similar kind of recommendation on the study of Phewa Lake which means the statement of the second hypothesis get an extra support on the validity of this study.

1.6 Limitations of the study

The study was limited by the budget constraints, time, weather, and a season of tourism that to get support from established literatures, transportation access location and transporting facilities available during visit, and other Environmental supports like weather, political conflicts etcetera, as the impacting factors to the Field survey. In addition, the field survey time was a seasons of land preparation to the farmers who was key point to provide the information as representatives of the community during the data collection process. The representatives' expertise and his/her motivation to expose the truth of questioning have also a major role to complete the study. Many representatives were provided hard time to involve in PRA (participatory Rural Appraisal) meeting in order to discuss with target people. Some subsequent appointments were re-organized. The concurrent political activities were not exceptional to delay the schedule of the interviews and a limited time with the tourists. On the time of gathering to the meeting, only limited people were interested to appear in interviews. During the meeting, many possible routes, sights, and viewpoints were suggested by local respondents and few of them were observed during the survey because the access to get a time. Few other locations were already known from my previous visit and experiences. More information about the local cultures and supporting factors for tourism were collected through the meeting and discussions with the local scholars.

Chapter II
Study area

2.1 Introduction

The city of Pokhara is situated about 200 km west of Katmandu (road distance) which is the second most important tourist destination of Nepal.

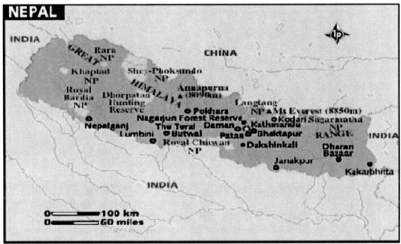

Source: http://www.lonelyplanet.com/maps/asia/nepal/

Geographically the valley occupies 625 sq km between the area of 83 58' 30" to 84 02' 30" east and 28 10' to 28 16' north and it is rounded by hillside villages by situating towards the south of Annapurna ranges. The fishtail is a peak of Annapurna Himalayas provides the extreme beauty of Pokhara from the approximate distance of 4 km to the valley. Dr. Horka (1990) described the geographical composition of Pokhara valley which is made from the tectonic movement of the glacier substances and the depth of the valley is situated at the height of 800 meter from the sea level.

Annapurna Ranges from the Kundahar, Pokhara.

The valley is mainly demarcated into Pokhara and Lekhnath municipalities. The neighboring areas for the tourism include some hillside villages such as Naudanda, Sarankot, Kaundanda, Dhampus, Nirmal Pokhari, Kalika, and the Sundaridanda. The five sampling spots in the study area were selected on the base of preliminary study of the local trekking areas among the view points. An attraction of the long Himalayan range and mountains toward the north of Pokhara valley highlights the importance to the nature visitors. The glomming bunches of Rhododendron flowers in the different patches of the stratified forests provides the panoramic beauty of Pokhara valley, seasonally. The lakeside is a famous tourists place belonging on the shore side of the Phewa Lake and as a part of city in the valley.

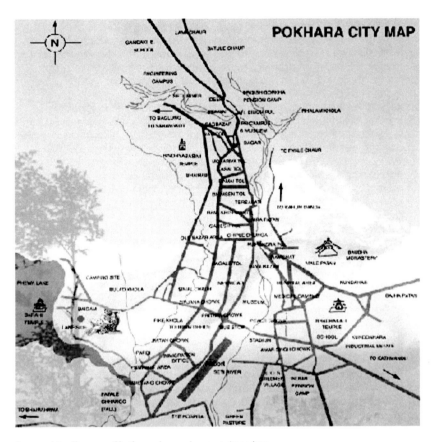

POKHARA CITY MAP

Source: http://www.go2kathmandu.com/concerto/map.htm

The total population of the valley is over 200 thousands and the city growth rate is 7.41% according to 2001 census, while the countryside villages was recorded below 50 thousands in total. Ethnically, culturally, and religiously, the region has rich diversified communities in the society. The valley is occupied by mixed communities of Hindus, Buddhists, Christians, and Muslims. There are many languages according to castes and religion, but most of the people can speak and understand Nepali, the national language of Nepal. City area is dominated by Gurung, Newar, and Thakali, among the many other castes. Many people have occupied some land for agriculture as the traditional occupation and handle side job to support the family income as the business or civil servants or in other fields. Some people have been conducting hotel or restaurant business since the tradition and some others recognizing as the farmer. In the latest days, many young people have a trend to move foreign countries to get the better job and income.

Regarding the culture, recreation, and in other activities in local levels, The people in the mountains have more traditional cultures in recreational activities such as in music, songs, and instrumentation, than in the city. The arts of music, traditional dresses, and cultural instruments have a high value and proudest in the tourist markets. Although, many of the arts of tradition printed in the musical instrumentation are not generalized in the market, yet. They are rare and diminishing condition due to a dominating phase of incoming cultures through foreign songs and languages and getting replacement to the trend of tradition, soon.
Culturally, a diversity of the people has an influenced of geo-climatic variation of the settlement. People of some areas are Buddhist and some other areas are Hindu. Many Hindus have a believe of god and goddess and also visits many temples of different Devi-devatas time to time and, as the festivals. Meanwhile Buddhists believe on Buddha Gumpa as the home of Buddha. Buddha has a respect and a historical importance to all the Nepali communities in the society.

2.2 Natural resources

The landmass of Pokhara region is associated with some natural resources such as Himalayas, Forests, Streams, Lakes and a Biological diversity. Many Himalayan peaks belong to the Annapurna ranges, and in lower level characterized as an impounded ecosystem with pristine nature of vegetation, and than the settlement of Human ecological relation, which has been characterized as the socio-culturally rich traditional villages in the countryside of the valley. More accurately, an ecologically accompanied diversified composition of beautiful forest with human settlement is highlighting to its value. The cost of ecological value to these residents is infinitive. According to Annapurna Conservation Area Project (ACAP)'s information, it is a richest area in the number of species of flora and fauna, in overall. Regionally, the ACAP have been starting for conservation activities towards the northern zone of the valley as the Annapurna project area. The Annapurna Conservation area is a highly diversified area of the wildlife, geography, and in culture. The combined environment of the nature as in the form of echo-adventure with the human settlement is the major ornaments of the attraction of this area.

Annapurna and Daulagiri peaks in Annapurna Ranges

According to ACAP museum in Pokhara, the diversity of the wildlife consists of 1126 species of flowering plants, 101 species of the mammals including red panda, musk deer, snow leopard etcetera, 474 species of birds, 41 species of reptiles, and 23 species of amphibians. It has some zoogeographical relation with flora and fauna, which could be an interesting tour to the world's nature scientists. The diversified rocks as the collection of the earth crusts are associated as a geographical history of the central Himalayan zone and it can provide an opportunity to study the earth science among the visitors. Similarly, the importance of the Himalayan vegetations and its' application in the area of science, medicine or for cosmetics has a high value for further production when use commercially. Many types of vegetation have the unique characteristics; color, smell, taste, and the nature. Therefore, an exploration of opportunities of the nature could be an important achievement to the visitors and to the local people.

Chapter III

Methodology of the study

3.1 Definition

The literatures study, questionnaire surveys, and field visits were the major tools to get the information and the data. During my field study, the preliminary data and several round of discussion were used with the academic representatives, community members, focus groups, and the tourists who were helpful to define different aspects of eco-tourism. The first field study was held in February and through March at 2002. Its additional resources were used to complete data by waiting extra time and events. Several other discussions were used for editing, writing and composing the report for scientific validation with few of my colleagues. The reports of the study basically concentrated on primary data, which was collected during observation, interviews, questionnaire surveys, group discussions and from PRA (Participatory Rural Appraisal) methods. The research is mainly based on assumption that to achieve a more holistic view of issues and a wider picture of the scenarios. This is a qualitative report on sustainable Ecotourism planning to improve the life standard and get support the liveliness of the people of that region.

The sampling sites were selected separately in the urbanized and non-urbanized areas. As many as trekking routs were expected to connect the view points during surveying, and sampled different expectations of the tourism in a trekking route on the base of objectives. Among the sampling sites Naudanda, Dhampus and kalikasthan were used as the two days trekking route and kanhuhill, sundaridanda, and sarankot were on the category of one day's route. Among the all, the household representatives were selected as the participants of the total household sampling design of each location. Questions, discussions, and the suggestions were used to collect information wisely.

As the urbanized parts, Pokhara and Lekhanath municipalities were divided into many sampling areas and used for primary data collection. Many hotels, restaurants, and lodges were represented as a sample for questionnaire survey and the collected information were as much as valid, true, and useful to support the strength of their capacity, if the question of employment, qualities, and standard of the hotel move in the

26

right direction. Except that, field study was successful to point out the situation of unmanaged city centers, parks, lakes and streams and also the problems of trekking agencies, guides, and the tourists in the Environment. The observations, discussions, questionnaire surveys, reports, and public interactions were the major resources to the information of the study and it was also helpful to analyze the impacts of the current political situation of the Environment.

3.2 Interviews:

The ideas of structured and semi-structured questionnaires were applied to gather detail information about the management and curiosity of new planning to the development of Ecological tourism, which could facilitate the management issues and lower the adverse impacts to the society and the tourists. During the interviewing time, an average number (10) of interested tourists were chosen to give answers each day. To make valid numbers of the representation and getting the central ideas of the tourists, they were selected to pick up from whole city, nearest trekking paths, and/ or hotels etcetera. Some semi-structured interviews were also designated to make flexibility in answering and suggest questioning to express in own ideas from the discussion for many representatives and the researchers. The purpose of the semi-structured interview could allow them to ask additional questions in an un-interactive discipline and it could let them to open an additional experience in that area.

The professional representatives to the designation of the surveys were selected among the trekking team leaders and guides' leader, and NGOs representatives who have been working in tourism development and nature conservation sectors. The additional (6) scholars were selected among the political representatives, the campus representatives and lecturers of the survey areas. All the locations for meeting were selected in a convenient place for majority people such as office, restaurant, and/ or to the open space. The direct interviews were requested mostly in one week advance and all the interviews were taking times over six and half weeks to the total time. An additional collection and correction of collected data were considered to the end of data selection time.

3.3 The Focus Groups' discussion

The people who had direct or indirect impact of the tourism to their daily lives and the representatives from that group were recognized as the responsible person of the group.

Social, Environmental, Professional, and academic sectors were included in the focus group. The Focus groups of people were used to extract key information that they would provide personal experiences, opinions, and demands in a certain issues of the topic. They also might express their own views, attitudes, and a concept to the value of tourism and its' impacts to the local communities. An the example, a focus group meeting among the trekking guides and travel agencies representatives of the Lake- sides were expressing own personal problem of the low salary issues and discontinuity in employment were made questioning to the current management of tourism of the country. Same opinions were provided by the travel agency representatives during the discussion. Both of the groups were agreed on some common problem in management and policy issues regarding the unmanaged trekking routes, security issues to the trekking members, benefit issues, service qualities, and an issue of information communication with the visitors.

In another one discussion with the local political representatives who were providing a mixed feelings about the negative or positive impacts of tourism but they expressed a positive and cooperative view towards the development of eco-tourism. They were committed to support ecological tourism activities, however, they confused to certainty of their leadership role, planning ability, and managing budget because it was hard for programming by them. Therefore in recent evaluation, the environment of the politics is uncooperative, worthless, or unpredicted and fragile as the past.

The participatory Rural Appraisal (PRA) methods were used in rural areas to identify the public emphasis to their own judgment about the current problems and for future developing schemes. PRA is easier to apply in homogenous people of the community than in a heterogeneous (diverse standard and expectation) communities of the cities. Rural area's people are less diverse and economically similar than with a town. It is more useful to apply PRA in rural villages than in the city. Therefore, same or similar standard could provide certainty to estimate an idea to the planning than in diverse, and PRA could be more useful in poor developing countries than in developed one.

3.4 Questionnaire surveys

Questionnaire survey was used to get additional information for management, workers training, and quality improvement, and developing skills in servicing sectors. Functionally, management in ecotourism development defines the wide areas of scheme that can provide appropriate service and an Environmental balance to the future needs. Management in trekking routes, view points, adventurous spots, hotels restaurants, security points, and an exhibition of cultural development in an economic world. More professionally, the ecology of the nature and the liveliness of local population should be upgraded in equilibrium of a natural balance which could enforce people to educate in Ecotourism development and an ecological conservation of the natural assets, both.

To get the support for sustainability to future, principle guidelines should be developed in planning, management, and implementation of laws and orders etcetera in times. There are many things to do including good administrative approaches in employee training, developing skills and increasing professionalism etcetera. In the tradition of business in Nepal, many of the rules and regulation get escape through the power handling personal and such domination of moral power does not scale the direction of right movement necessary to establish for necessary trend. So far the understanding of the tradition of system is one of the important messages to the sustainability developer in a new developing plan. Regarding the standardized quality and skills, there have been found few practices in certain level in the private hotel sectors but it is not enough to support an uniformity with another private parties of another location. Therefore, they need a practical course of training to enforce uniformity in quality, skills and facilities. The questionnaire surveys were also focus to such information that would help to develop a clear vision in the new policy. In the field survey, the questionnaire was distributed to the 45 hotel representatives (as the sampling number) but 34 of them were returned as the responded answers.

3.5 Literatures Study

During the time of literature study, the definition of sustainable eco-tourism composed by ECOMOST project (1994) was focused as a reference which provides two important points as the model of sustainable tourism. *"First, sustainability is no threat to tourism and it should assume the profitable future of tourism. Second, sustainability is related to natural environment and is more specially referred to as the ecology"*. In addition, the ECOMOST project focuses the principle in three sectors for sustainable development such as in Ecological sustainability, Cultural and social sustainability, and Economic sustainability. The most important united slogan of the world wide attention is in the prospective of sustainable development of eco- tourism today. Pokhara region has a high scope of natural beauty and god gifted resources that are valuable to attract tourism, and it is necessary to manage ecological tourism to continue its sustainability.

In today's world, there are some more acceptable concepts of modern tourism worldwide; the principle of Agenda 21 states a strong support to the ecotourism which provides an opportunity to the local community as the needs of natural environment without any damage by human beings. *"Sustainable ecotourism is an application of a combining idea of the nature conservation and development as the prospective of Ecotourism (WTTC et al 1996)"*. The modern acceptable literatures of ecotourism are more valuable to the data collection and to improve the confidence of the study in the field of ecological tourism in Nepal.

In the history of modern tourism in Nepal, it was started since 1951 when Nepal opened its boarder for foreigners (visitors, officials, business man, and scholars) from the drawn of democracy after Rana Regime. After the succession of the democratic movement of 1951, Nepal started to open diplomatic relation with many other countries in the addition of India and China. Since that, Nepal has been extending its friendship and openness in the world.

When Tenzing Sherpa and Edmund Hillary were scaled the peak of the Mount Everest (8848m height) in 1953, Nepal first recognized as a famous worldwide, meanwhile the tourism started to grow continue as the business.

The formal history of tourism planning in government sector has been introduced since 1956 and a trend of five years development plans have been started through the planning commission to establish the new infrastructure for growing tourism. Some of the changes happening step by steps by times, but in practical the development has not been made satisfaction to getting the new opportunities in the country. Many new governments and developers proposed new planning on the tourism but it didn't bring any measurable changed to the need of the demand for a long time. Lack of vision for sustainability in tourism, created financial problems by monarchy, and corruptions could be a main reason to obstruct the development. There might be some others latest environmental problems such as the political un-stability, a continued corruption in administrative level, unpredicted population growth, lack of appropriate education in the sustainability etcetera, could be the recent barriers of eco-tourism development in Pokhara.

Reviewing the literatures, there are some research reports published by ICIMOD, IUCN, Annapurna Conservation Area Project (ACAP) and few others from government officials. Many they were made to fulfill the formality of research as the requirement of the project and few of them are comparatively better. Anyway, the findings of many reports have been focusing to the human encroachment in the lakes and to the unmanaged pollution of the city. The study of the reports has been continuing to aware the situation of the worsening environment. The challenges are increasing day by days, while a power of leadership has no appropriate direction to check up the situation from further worsening. As the conclusion, Pokhara region needs a project to develop a sustainable ecotourism integrated package in a new planning and management scheme.

Chapter IV

Study Analysis

4.1 Data collection

As the finding of the interviews with tourists and studied literatures, many foreign tourists visit Nepal either for adventure tourism in order to enjoy the height of the mountains or for academic purposes in study and research. But many of them visit Pokhara to spent leisure time of the holiday or vacation. Some of the visitors define their aim of world visit and they believe Nepal is an un-avoided place to travel among the important others. There is one important comment by third counties' visitors that the plane ticketing system is less facilitates to purchase and hard to exchange the flight in case if they needed to shift their time for intruding Nepal. Except the intruders from the neighboring countries, rest of the tourists has to use air plane service to entering Nepal, through the Capital Katmandu and the visit move towards the destination and objectives of the program.

Pokhara region is one of the important trekking zones to the foreigners among the other trekking areas of Nepal. A trend of attraction towards Pokhara is further increasing among the visitors. As a comparison as for example, during the first decades of the opening to the outer world in Nepal, more than one hundred expeditions from sixteen countries arrived to climb the challenging Himalayan peaks. Between 1960 to 1970 the number of foreign visitors traveling Nepal increased just over 4000, and it was over 445,000 by the end of the decade 1999 (statistics record book 2000). On the mean time, Pokhara visiting numbers were recorded since 1980 to 1999 and the trend of development was as the table no 2.

Table: 2, A History of tourists' records since 1980 to 2000, in Pokhara.

Year	Total arrived in Pokhara	Arrived by plane	Arrived by roads	Annual variation %
1980	33161	6532	26629	-
1981	34725	5661	29064	4.7
1982	34990	5912	29073	0.8
1983	32234	6221	26013	-7.9
1984	35329	5548	29781	9.6
1985	36577	6101	30476	3.5
1986	39439	6482	32957	7.8
1987	50275	10478	39797	27.5
1988	58112	14636	43476	15.6
1989	65105	11756	53349	12.0
1990	59488	9344	50144	-8.6
1991	62138	15065	47073	4.5
1992	69049	16876	52173	11.1
1993	56499	15966	40533	-18.2
1994	59201	20548	38653	4.8
1995	63782	21262	42520	7.7
1996	86504	26044	60460	35.6
1997	92717	29471	63246	7.2
1998	103895	36320	67575	12.1
1999	105546	68243	37303	1.2
2000	95095	61812	33283	-9.9
2001	93731			-1.4

Source: Data recorded by tourism office Pokhara and provided by Tourism department, The Ministry of civil aviation, Kathmandu (2002).

The history of the tourists flow up to 1999 shows a steady growth and than interrupted by dropping the visits by the Maoists' insurgency in the country. The proportion of unstable numbers will take time to settle by extra few years when peaceful environment set up.

4.2 Month-wise tourist's arrival in Pokhara

Table 3: Month wise tourists' arrived

Month	Tourists in 1996	Tourists in 1997	Tourists in 1998	Tourists in 1999	Tourists in 2000	Tourists in 2001	Total in 5 years
Jan	7825	8386	9089	9543	8596	11083	54532
Feb	8204	8336	9513	10054	9053	11520	56680
Mar	9152	9953	11758	12381	11154	112953	67351
Apr	9669	10239	11127	11683	10549	11353	64620
May	5290	6666	8205	7509	6761	1256	35687
Jun	2451	2914	3479	3571	3214	3005	18634
Jul	3314	3781	4182	3980	3585	2818	21661
Aug	4597	5894	6368	6700	6038	3368	32965
Sept	6440	7383	7973	8291	7465	4004	41556
Oct	11143	10902	11714	11563	10460	9727	65509
Nov	8878	10180	10993	9545	9700	9328	58624
Dec	9543	8083	9493	9545	8520	5316	50500
Total	86504	92717	103895	105546	95094	93731	568319

Source: Tourism office Pokhara; Feb 2002.

By comparing the data of the table no. 3 the incoming ratio of the foreign tourists are following estimation as in the bar graph, every month.

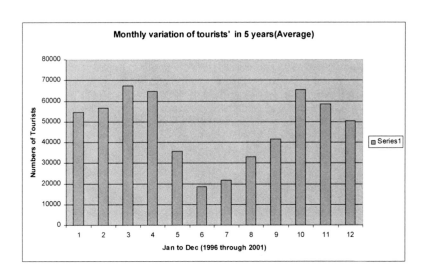

4.3 <u>Country-wise Foreign Visitors arrived in Pokhara.</u>

Table 4: Visitors from foreign Countries

Year	Germany	Japan	UK	USA	France	Australia	Other Foreigners
1991	5145	7634	7778	4923	3281	4112	29264
1992	6789	6363	9847	5534	4221	3947	32348
1993	5400	5193	8096	5000	3290	4408	25112
1994	4378	5378	6677	5117	3030	3515	31106
1995	5657	6027	7812	5307	3617	4606	30756
1996	7687	7329	10790	7324	5043	6234	42097
1997	9018	9077	12296	8716	5754	6993	40863
1998	10094	10606	15302	9181	6101	8165	44146
1999	9500	11304	14850	9251	5810	8070	46761
2000	8911	11606	14743	9100	5329	7895	37511
2001	7352	14542	10951	7728	4496	2114	21504
Total	79931	95059	119143	77481	49972	60059	381468

Field survey 2002; data from the tourism office, Pokhara.

The number of tourists arrived in Pokhara between 1991 to 2001 indicates a mixed result; the numbers of visitors from all of the countries' were increasing gradually up to 1998 and then dropping down except Japan that means Japanese tourists are less affected with the insurgency of the Maoist's movement. The most logical reason for affecting visitors could be by the underground insurgency of the Maoists' activities and its' impact in the tourism. There are also some other reasons to scare the visitors were as an unstable activities of the government and a lack of security guaranty in the tourists.

4.4 Purpose of visit in Pokhara

During the time of interview, many of the tourists representatives defined their purpose why they were choosing to Pokhara for their visit, were as the followings:

Table 5: Objectives of the Pokhara visits:

SN	Nationality of the foreigners	World trekking purpose	Recreation & business	Holiday pleasure	Mountaineering	Research
1	India (20)	5	2	10	2	1
2	UK (12)	8	-	2	-	2
3	Japan (10)	6	-	-	4	-
4	USA (4)	-	-	2	-	2
5	Germany (3)	3	-	-	-	-
6	Australia (3)	-	-	3	-	-
7	Others (37)	12	2	13	5	5
	Total	34	4	30	11	10

Source: Field survey, 2002.

Above table defines that the majority of Pokhara visitors were visiting for holiday pleasure and world trekking purpose and the others were for recreational, study, and for mountain trekking purposes. Therefore, the planning and policies of the tourism development should consider the demand of the market towards the priority of the visitors. Definitely the market is competitive and the world trekkers could be visit again if they get better accessibility and enjoyable environment than other worlds. To get the better environment to the trend of tourism, the decade of 2010 is already passing and looking forwards to the success of peaceful environment in Nepal.

4.5 Infrastructures & employment capacity in Tourism

Pokhara region has a huge capacity to use the beauty of Nature. The need of the infrastructural development for tourism is not in estimation yet, because the current situation in tourist facilities is insufficient to the growing businesses. There are not any new planning for infrastructural or any other adventurous development to extending tourism in government level but the capacity building and developing infrastructure is an important step to start a developing plan, today. Therefore, the capacity building should support to increase business, employment situation, awareness in ecological conservation and an upgrading economy in local people. But any of the activities related to tourism business will not helpful to get long term benefit, if that is contradicted with the aim of ecotourism sustainability principle.

As a conclusion, the capacity buildings in tourism management such as for hotel management and developing trekking facilities are always important to establish in the poor developing country like Nepal. The countryside or villages are more attractive than the city's environment of the urbanized areas in Pokhara, while the remote villages have no such infrastructural management like the city has.

4.51 Lodging capacity and Employees

According a sampling of the hotel sectors, there are several types of employees on the base of categories and responsibilities, such as part-time, seasonal or on regular basis. The working fields of the tourism employees are mainly divided into trekking fields, coordinating for travels, lodging and hotels, and as the restaurant workers. Some of the employees are used to work for cleaning, house keeping, cooking, catering, recreation, and for a safe guard (protection) etcetera. But the ratio of men and women workers has an inequality in employment sector according to the concurrent data of the hotel employees.

Table 6: Employee's ratio in the Hotel sector:

Gender	Employees in the star hotels			Employees in the non star hotels			Total employees	Aggre gated %
	Sample number	Total estimated	%	Sample number	Total estimated	%		
Female	32	75	10	91	728	30	803	23.76
Male	288	672	90	225	1670	70	2342	76.24
total	320	747	10	316	2398	100	3145	100

Source: A Sample Field survey February 2002.

According to the survey of 2002, 272 Hotels and Resorts in the Pokhara metropolis were specially expanded after 1980s and the numbers developed drastically after re-establishment of the democracy in Nepal at 1989. According to the study resources, only the 14 stars and 258 non stars hotels were providing a capacity of lodging for 6,387 tourists every day and 3145 employees as a regular job in Pokhara vicinity.   Most of the hotels in Pokhara provide feeding and lodging facilities to the guests. Few other hotels were offering food, lodging and restaurant services to the tourists.

Many of the hotels' employees were worked either as the family members or through a personal reference of the relatives, and rest of the employees might be professional as a cook, drivers, cleaners or others. Sometimes, the owner has to take overall responsibilities of the work, sometimes.

Many hotels, lodges and restaurant have a un-equality in the ratio of female employees with the ratio of male employees. During the survey, the percentage of the women in the star hotels and non-star hotels were only 10 to 30. The total average of the female employees was recorded about 23.76% only. This data indicates a constraint of the gender issue and the biasness to the women. During the study, the reason of the biasness was questioned to the local authorities, representative of the hotel association, and to the local scholars, separately. The reasons of the biasness were estimated as the following three different points:

1. Since the tradition, the role of women were used as a home makers and many family women members don't like to work in hotels' servicing job because an undervaluation by responsibilities.
2. Women are traditionally less educated and less confident to work in hotels as the outside fields to the comparison of men.
3. Vulnerability of sexual exploitation to women in the hotel industry due to a week mechanism of government to protect the right of individuals especially for girls or women and it could be an impact of the tradition of male dominated society over women.

Here as the analysis, to meet the requirement of sustainability it is an urgent issue to create equality in the environment of work place between man and woman. Without any equal involvement of the women, the notion of the sustainable development will not fulfill its objectives and the sustainability of ecotourism finally undergoes diminishing.

The society and government most develop a suitable environment to involve the women participation openly and fearlessly. The creation of sustainability network and a development in the traditional socio-cultural environment is really a challenging question to the management of Nepal. By developing sustainability factors through the ecological tourism could help to narrow down the gap in the traditional differences of the gender issues.

4.52 Trekking and Camping Environment

 During the field observation, most of the trekking routes in the remote hilly areas were connected to the locally made paths to go to view points, and campsites. Some of the routes were passes through the private lands and also through the cattle trekking combined routs. Depending on the locality and a tradition of the family background, many people usually keep some cattle such as buffalos, cows, goats, sheep or pigs in their shed or land. Some remote mountainous people keep their sheep, horses or buffalos in the tundra forest of the high altitude. Some people use domestically trained dogs to take care animals, home or crops as the security purposes. The dogs are supposed to use for protecting crops from wild animals mostly monkeys. The campsites are usually estimated in a free peaceful land outside the residential area. That means the trekking guides estimate the spots at a peaceful location where is an un-interactive distance from the villagers. Trekking guide is very important factor to decide the location of campsites and choose safe trekking routes because there are no any organized or well managed routes or camping spots in every location. Trekking leaders also have to decide the sheltering time, weather condition, resource availabilities, and team safety in the camping zone to get the rest for camping night. Trekking guides are fully responsible to take care to the team during the whole trekking time depending on the availability of the facilities, etcetera. Many trekking routes and camp sites need an improvement to facilitate the tourists. Pollution management and treatment is an important work for collected traces and created pollution in a proper way.

Many places of the camping sites are temporary spots and mostly for one night stay and not for summer. Camping and trekking on the same schedule plan is more enjoyable among the trekking groups. Trekking is used continuing for many days and the camping areas are usually changing in different location in the open spaces. Mountains, valleys, villages, and forests are the major parts of the trekking routes. Trekking towards the height of the mountain and an open long range of scenario of the Himalayan peaks provides an enjoyment of the peaceful nature.

The different forests' patches of the altitudes and a mix farming system of the local communities make an unimaginative feeling to the western countries' visitors. Most of the people of Pokhara region have some cropping land to grow their food whatever they needed to the whole year. They usually have some cattle such as cows, buffalos, goats, sheep, or chicken. The high altitude crops like wheat, millet, oat, maize or potatoes are the major production of that region and some others varieties are also used to cropping as their needs. Sometimes, it could be an exceptional study to the foreign sociologists about the residential pattern and a socio-economic life style of the remote habitants which could provide an extra memory or knowledge among the visitors.

The cultural isolation due to geographical remoteness and diversities, traditional life styles, and a genetic differentiation in the local mountainous communities have so many characteristics and messages to the Biological, sociological researchers. Due to reason of geographical remoteness in the mountains, many people have never been visited outside their territory, and they never been touch with the city, or never been seen roads, motors, shopping centers, and other major development of the modern world. Many of these people might be poor in facilities, but never weak in the feeling of dignity and mind, and are strong in their unity and moral characters of the humanism.

In some trekking routes, you will get some resting place (locally called Chautaro) where the trekking guides, porters and tourists could used as the resting plate forms during trekking. The Chautaros are usually made by local religious people with the help of communities according to their tradition. In most of the old trekking routes the resting plate forms are found in certain distance and they are usually with two different cultural trees (Pipal & Bar) to provide the shadow to the trekkers. This kind of plate forms are constructed in a religious believes and as the social service since the tradition. In Nepal, many villages and mountainous trekking routes are such a rich in development and believes. Resting plate forms are popular and more helpful in the societies since the history.

A trekking could provide an opportunity to see traditional villages of the mountainous sides. The reasons of diversified tradition could be protected by a geographical remoteness and an isolation of the language, cultures and traditions which could provide an expensive experience to the foreign visitors depending on how the remoteness and the tradition of the castes diversifying in the communities. In Pokhara vicinities, the majority of the mountainous communities are dominated by Gurung who are culturally rich, and specified in own language, traditions and in social activities. The second dominated castes of the societies are Brahman, Chhetrie, Thalami, and the thirds are other caste of people of the societies. Cultures and traditions are valuable and important to the study purposes.

The developing possibilities for many of the adventurous scenarios like a Kaligandaki gorge and the nearest traveling distance of the Annapurna peaks from the city of Pokhara has an opportunity of a future development to connect by a cable car which could be a highly demanded achievement of the future tourism industry of Pokhara.

4.53 Infrastructures & Tourism

Guests are gods in Nepali culture and tourists are the guests to Nepali people.
There is a mutual relationship between providers and accepters to establish a market of the tourism in a natural environment in the world.

Currently, Pokhara has both private and government involvements to build the infrastructural development such as hotels, restaurants, roads, and the recreational areas. The government efforts are invested mostly in offices, roads, schools and colleges, hospitals and in some recreational spots such as Mahendra Gupha (Cave), David fall (water spring) and so on. There are also some local involvement as the volunteering support to make roads, schools, colleges, and offices by local people for some instance.
In the private sectors, people are investing own private money and time in hotel or Restaurant as the owner and also as an employee to improve their own business with a developing trend of competition of that region. Public investments are also high in transportation sectors to buying buses and taxis' which are the key element to get the trekking fields. In addition, there is also some private investment as a cooperative business like the trekking, traveling and ticketing agencies to facilitate the visitors and get their destiny in time. In Pokhara vicinities, there are many public activities have been willingly proving a support to the tourism industry and forcing government to celebrate the Nepal visit year ...time to times in tourism era. Some of the latest arrangement for paragliding and ultra plane flying activities are continuing efforts of the private sectors and are taking tourist market since the decades.

The qualities and accessibilities of the services are limited due to many reasons because the progress of poor developing country of the world. Rural hillsides are more inconvenience to use communication, transportation and to get other facilities for passengers. In many places, there is no electricity, internet and any other facilities like the urbanized area. But you get a peace, pleasure and adventure of the nature, if you succeed to get a right destiny on the beauty of climax. To get an extreme enjoyment and pleasure there are some key factors to managing your trekking program such as your team members, trekking schedule, selection of trekking route, planning of time and season of the climates and the team guides who will provide you an guidance, help, and leadership to get the destiny in more easy and enjoyable way. These were some major challenging factors to the visit.

To get an extreme adventure of nature, the transportation is a really difficult problem because many more isolated geographical areas are really remote, inaccessible by trekking routes but unique, and a remote human habitation in the surroundings. *As a remarkable memory, I have my self experienced of Dudh Pokhari (a sanctuary) trekking, which is belonged to the southwest of the Manasolu Himalayas in Lamjung district. It is a beautiful natural as well as religious trekking place with a seasonally colorful sanctuary surrounded by many medicinal and aromatic plants and with many different colors of Rhododendron flowers and so on. We enjoyed lots with a feeling of total affiliation of the mind on the sole of nature and extreme nature. End of the day, my team decided to get down Bhirpustoon, by traveling through a remote village called Naizar. During traveling, we met the head of the villager (called Mukhiya in Nepali on the way); while I tried talk some things to know about their lifestyles. But we were just able to understand few things. I estimated few stone made houses on the steps of the mountain for their sheltering and with no patio or boundary in style. Few of the people including children might were looking us with the dress like animal's skin probably from the deer. Land like cropping areas was observed with oats, looked the people spent night with the burning woods, and get food mostly wild animals, fried oat's paste and natural vegetables. The eye catching distance from the Bahundanda to this location is not far (may be 3 miles) because a single land mass of the hillside of the mountain separated by a slopping landmass and a stream of snow water called Nyadee. We wouldn't be imagined how the life spending in that isolated society of human settlement could. It was my private visit with few of my colleagues who were guided me through an un-imaginative trekking route at 1985. During the trekking I were familiar with some others villages like Chipla, Tarachock, and Syange which are associated with an ecology of the nature and more organized in life settlement and in culture.*

Do we imagine how adventurous traveling could be, if a network of Cable car could planned to connect mountain to mountains and isolated to isolation of the nature, etcetera?

Chapter V
Major Constraints in tourism

To assess the data from questionnaire surveys, field observations, literatures study, interviews and so on, there were some important constraints to the development of Ecotourism and its sustainability as the followings:

5.1 Constraints Studies

The private sectors and their investments are dominated in hotels and restaurants business. The field study collected data from questionnaire survey also included the findings of women bios employment in many fields; in hotels, trekking fields, and in driving areas. It means the un-equality could be originated through a tradition that the women have to work only at home and it has not been accepted if women go to outsides' the home in society. The tradition of male dominated history has a male sex supporting culture which might be unevaluated bios society and it has been suffering from male dominated psychology since the history. Continuing in the present, there is a strong vulnerability of sexual exploitation of women workers in hotels, lodges, and others similar fields. The additional region of less women workers in driving and trekking fields voiced the general answer as male are strong to handle outsides works and female are not strong to fulfill the responsibilities and less secured than male. The constraints of the society as the tradition of male dominated culture could be an obstacle for gender equality in the development of women employment. The planning of sustainable ecotourism will not complete its objectives if half of the population (women) has been surviving in the shadow of male dominated tradition.

In recent days, some social awareness programs have been warning a sound for equality between man and women (Ref: Nepali local news) but these were not enough to implement as the law and orders. It is essential to bring up the program in the society which could make enough protection, education and encouragement of equality in the daily life of the women. Therefore, the new policy of tourism should include the gender equality vision in the sustainable ecotourism planning program for Pokhara region.

Another constraint to the sustainability program has been affecting by the foreign dependency in food production, clothes and developing infrastructural resources especially from India. India is a big country surrounding to Nepal by the boarders of east, west and the south. Year by Years, Indian media such as TV, news, and advertises are dominating over the Nepalese media. Since the last three decades, Nepali government has been allowing Indian TV Channels as a shadow negotiation that means, Nepalese people are motivated to learn Indian cultures, languages, and advertises and should not develop their own culture, language and business of Nepal! Day by days, Nepal has been demanding a huge proportion of food products such as chickens, meet, vegetables, Rice and so on; a varieties of construction materials such as cements, Iron, marbles, paints, working tools, parts of building materials, and fibers; the home supply items such as mattresses, cotton beds, utensils, clothes, make up, and medicines etcetera. The other type of items such as electronics, ready made cloths, and leather items etcetera has been supplying from China, Hung Kong, and Singapore and from other parts of the world. The questions to the Nepali societies, political parties, and the government: *where is the development status of Nepal and how long does it takes to return into an independent sovereign country?*

If we assess the payment to the foreign goods, a huge amount of the national investment has been loosing its money for daily needs and for luxurious items. It is suppose to compare with a vessel which has a hole on the bottom but you have to bring up water from the river to survive your friends and family, you don't repair the leaking vessel and you will dream the high pitch slogan for independency, extreme development to get equal facilities and similarly to sustainable ecotourism! There is big hole to stop leaking and a huge step to get success to achieve sustainability in every point.

There is a question on the way: How are the possibilities to develop and increase national production in the fields of agriculture, construction resources, medicines and others? How is the possibility to develop independency on the quality of national TV channels? How are the possibilities to protect Nepali culture and languages from foreign interferences? How far are the possibilities to develop modern technologies in resources preparation and employment generation in the sectors of construction and getting supports from a mutual relation of the developed countries? Yes, there are many challenges to influence the sustainability for development and it is important to start a planning and management of self dependency in ecotourism development in targeted part of the country and in whole nation.

According to the study of Ecotourism development planning report of IUCN (2000) in Lekhanath municipality, there were many constraints to make the barrier for ecotourism development movement and one of the major things is cooperation among the local political forces and unification of local government body, but the Pokhara metro had a unsatisfactory cooperation according to survey of Lekhanath Municipality. In which, Lekhanath municipality has introduced an ecotourism planning model by a slogan of ecotourism development plan as "A garden city of seven lakes", and this area belongs to a part of Pokhara valley. The Begnas, Rupa, Khaste, Dipang, Gunde, Neureni, and Maidee are in the group of seven lakes. Many of them have a serious siltation problem and public encroachment due to an open exploitation activities in the past. During the time of discussion (2002), the mayor Mr. S. R. Adhikari were explaining the commitment proposal that they were ready to lunch the planning if political parties unanimously help to manage Ecotourism planning and development in that municipality. Therefore, political differences and misunderstanding is also a major constraint to the development activities in tourism of Pokhara region.

5.2 Awareness to the visitors

There are few other challenges overcome during the times of trekking and camping, such as to aware to the visitors in the trekking routes, providing necessary help to the week members if troubled, providing right information and additional guidance if required in local level, providing security issues, and providing safety training during visit, etcetera. Depending on the size of team, the trekking guides should organize the timeline and capacity of camping site and to manage to exhibit local assets which could be interesting to that group.

Regarding the situation of trekking sites, most of the trekking route is remote and difficult to identify, which means there are many chances of misguidance and time line problems to the travelers. If one time missed to their trekking trek than they will need help for more information. If the local helping person suggested something that might be inaccurate or wrong information and a kind of trouble happens. Most of the times you will get help from any one local people but occasionally, bad people can provide wrong suggestions to your trekking path. This kind of problem could happen, especially if you are traveling only one, two or just three without any true guidance or the details of trekking information. Security situation in the country is un-protective, sometime un-effective and incapable in remote areas of mountainous region. There are also dangerously remote places, very attractive by the nature, deep dove or

stream, huge boulder and sometimes step rocks which are hard to get
success for trespassing. And again, the traveler could be exhausted and
tired to get the destiny.
Many of the tragedies or misbehaviors happen if some bad followers or
trickery has been following you. You never know who is who but you can
stop your journey until you can't trust. It is better to make big trekking
group than an individual to go to trekking to the point of safety. When you
are trekking alone, be aware with irrelevant helper who looks bad
intentionally and try motivating unnecessary to you.

During an interview one of the visitor from western countries explained his
experiences about a misbehave of a stranger when they were trekking
with a group of five people, and they needed to get help to make sure
which one is the right trek on a subdivided trekking route. While a young
man came up and showed to catch the right hand trek to go to the
Karaputar Lamjung from Begnas. The trek was directed down slop
through a forest, and move straight left. According to interviewee, they
were followed up to the same suggested trek but few minutes later, few
stones and pebbles made falling on the trekking path where they were
walking. Fortunately, nobody heart from that attack or accident. It was so
confusion about whom, and why, the silly misbehave doing. Was it
possible, the same strange person who was provided direction to them
made stones falling? But as a conclusion, the visitor explained his
enjoyment of the round trip and said, "It was so scary on that day but I like
to visit those mountains, again".

In conclusion, the constraints could be minimized through some extra
practices, for example by the direction of Education, news and
communication, and using protection mechanism and so on, to support
the Eco-tourism development in Nepal. In addition, developing
educational management and providing an opportunity to open eyes in
an ecotourism benefits in local environment by establishing ecotourism
media to solve the problems or challenge to the sustainability of
Ecotourism development to that region.

5.3 Impacts of tourism

Environmental pollution, soil erosion, deforestation and cultural exploitation could be major negative impacts in the locals and in the society of Pokhara region.

The city area is facing two types of tourism problems, in fact, the internal and foreign tourists. The internal tourists are mainly religious pilgrims, official travelers, recreational travelers and business man from the other parts of the country. There has been some unusual interaction of different prospective of the people in the society which could emphasize to the sexual interference, and girls trafficking in the environment. The over crowded people and an unmanaged mass tourism can increase additional pollution and exploitation to the city.

As the negative impact of the tourists, there has been serious attack to the Nepali cultures and languages from the foreigners more seriously from neighboring country like India and less from others like Pakistan, Bangladesh, western countries etcetera. The cultures and media policy of Indian government has domination with free interacting policy to others. The government of Nepal is incapable to protect Nepali language and culture because the Indian channels are open to the Nepali media and the Indian tourists prefer to communicate mostly in Hindi and get enjoyment by Hindi songs over international or Nepali songs and culture. The factor to invite Indian culture by some Nepali workers in India, who had habitual to Hindi and have no any cultural awareness or education that to save own cultures. The additional things of the cultural attack being made from the Indian business man and immigrated workers who are dominating the foot path of Nepali market specially in major cities like Katmandu, Pokhara, Biratnagar, Bhairawa etcetera. It is unbearable things to any one true Nepali who love own ethics, cultures, and morality. Beyond these impacts, few other impacts were noted from third countries' tourists especially from Europe, Australia, and America. The developed countries tourists usually have less interaction by numbers, frequencies, and other behaviors etcetera. But there are some cultural impacts as the examples such as through open sexual activities in the public areas which is not the culture of Nepali societies.

The additional impacts in natural Environment are noted as the result of visitors such as the empty cans and bottles in the trekking fields and an impact in the forest to getting fire woods for cooking and heating the camping sites areas where they do stay whole night. Also another impact made by trekking groups such as soil compaction, and erosion were recorded in some trekking routes.

48

As the positive Impacts, people who have establishing a business and work in tourism fields, they are generating money and getting benefits by the competition in services.

5.4   Resulting immigrants' as an Impact

According to the population census (1997), there is a higher percentage of population growth in the lakeside in Pokhara due to an opportunity of the tourism business every year. The Lakeside has been suffering from poor infrastructures and by unsystematic settlement (NCSIP, 1997), which has an unplanned land uses and a high growth rate of population (7.41 %) every year, (Rastra Bank's research report 2001). Many of the growing population are the result of immigrants, mostly from neighboring villages and also from other parts of the country. Phewa Lake is highly polluted through the domestic sewages more seriously in east- south and an effect of erosion and unprotected pollution from the north- east.

Chapter VI
Conclusion and Recommendations

6.1 <u>Conclusion</u>

Pokhara Region needs an appropriate action plan to step up the sustainable Ecotourism development because the challenging situation of Ecological tourism has been loosing its future from the history in local, national and worldwide level.

A suitable Ecotourism management could be helpful to develop a mutual relationship between the ecology of nature and the human activities, as for example, the clean and healthy lake's water can support the future development of eco-tourism in the harmony of nature, if a continue investment for lake ecology improved.

Pokhara region has many possibilities for developing new opportunities of ecotourism. As the supporting factors; it has many ecological assets, geographical appropriateness, historical and cultural supports as the needs of people in the local level. In contrasts, it is challengeable to protect the vulnerability of damaging ecology from political conflicts, environmental pollution, gender un-equality, poor infrastructural management, and lack of environmental education in people towards the future sustainability.

The accesses of sewage passing drainages and unmanaged solid waste dumping sites in the lakes and River, and some other unjustifiable temporary plastic houses, might be the sources of ugliness to the city.

It is also important to meet the challenges of current tourism requirements such as protection, quality and management to develop the future profile of ecotourism in Pkhara region. The planning and management should not only direct to the short term benefit but also to develop for long term sustainability. Public participation in infrastructural development, planning to protect ecological assets; natural environments, geographical sites, and cultures are the policy factors to the development.

Therefore, there is a need of effective planning and integrated management for the development of sustainable ecotourism in Pokhara region.

6.2 Recommendations

A management needs a huge improvement through a strong policy and planning towards the enthusiasm of new direction of ecotourism development which could be a solution to the above problems.

Or

All kinds of national forces, societies, scholars, and individual people should get united to make an integrated development program as the revolution in Ecotourism development in Pokhara as well as in other feasible part of the country. In addition, the authority should work with local communities, user groups such as the people of the hotel and restaurant association, travel and trekking agencies, and with eco-tourism experts.

As the suggestions, to design and apply a development policy as the project, the following innovative actions could be taken.

- Every plan for development should be geared through sustainability principles; by balancing people's participation, ecological improvement, infrastructural development, equal opportunity to involvement in the activities of cultural development, employment and qualities etcetera.
- Ecotourism development is gradual process and it should be carried out within the limit of local infrastructures, carrying capacity, and time limit and investment of the project.
- The development policy should include the local, regional, and national level of the project that are necessary to design for different aspect of the tourism by using the importance of sustainable environment.
- The project should establish a revenue collection mechanism that need to use for developing natural sites, adventurous sites, trekking routes, developing education, and other assets that are further useful for environmental conservation and developing further activities to upgrading ecotourism sustainability.
- All kinds of required facilities should manage in the trekking routes, campsites, and at recreational places including developing activities in the arts.
- It should provide extra safety and protection system to the visitors, when they are participating in any tourism activities.

- The designation of national plan covers the cable car trekking unit as an adventure of beauty.
- Should be managed equal right to women and to manage reasonable salary system to each works.
- The legal framework should be developed to control the encroachment problems and punishment should be strong if any body violates the rules of protection plan.
- Clear rules and regulation have to be made to apply laws and orders strongly.
- Monitoring in sustainability in ecological tourism has to be review time to time and should precede further steps in each measure.

7. <u>Meaning of the words in Nepali (Glossary):</u>

Pokhara = Name of a city of the western region of Nepal.

Annapurna = Name of Inner Himalayas which is associated with Fishtail and few other peaks. Annapurna is also recognized as the god of grain in Nepali tradition.

Gayaa = Name of a religious place of India.

Kapilvastu = A Nepali ancient place where Buddha was Born.

Shankaracharya = the name of Hindu ideological leader selected since the ancient history of India.

Tenzing Norgey Sherpa = A Name of the person who climbed Mt Everest first time in the world's history.

Rana = Name of a cast of Nepal who were using the power of Nepal up to 104 years during the time of Shah Kingdom.

Prithvi = First Shah King in Nepal, who started to unify many small kingdoms into Big Nepal.

Dhaulagiri = A name of the peak of Annapurna Himalayan ranges.

Lamjung, Gorkhas, Tanahu, Sangjha = Name of some districts of Nepal.

Muktinath = A religious place that belongs to inter Himalayan zone of Nepal.

Dashain = A main festival of Hindu religion in Nepal.

Shalikgram = A stone supposed to used as the symbol of God in Hinduism.

53

Coriolis = Name of the earth creating inertial force, according to French mathematicians' explanation in 19 the century.

Phewa = or Fewa, a name of lake of Pokhara city.

Baraaha, Vindabashini, Bhadrakali = Name of the typical goddess of Hindu and their temple area.

Kalika = Name of a village of the Pokhara vicinity.

Gumpa = Home of Buddha and a praying center for Buddhists'

Kaligandaki = name of a river in the deep gorge of mountain

Siltation = Settling of sand and soil at the mouth of streams which displace water body and make a mass of silted land in that area.

Naudanda, Sarankot, Kaudanda, Dhampus, Nirmal Pokhara, Kalika, Sundaridanda = Name of the villages where camping sites, and trekking areas are set.

Devidevattas = Meaning of goddess in Nepali

Lekhanath = Name of an urbanizing (municipality) area of the Pokhara valley.

Gurung, Newar, Thakali, Bramhan, Chhetri, Magar, Sherpa = define castes, and cast is recognized mostly by family name and by subfamily names.

Begnas = Name of the Lake and the name of the village from the recognition of that lake.

Mahendra = A name given to a Cave by the name of Former King of Nepal.

Machhapuchhre = name of Fishtail peak which belongs to the
Annapurna Himalaya of Nepal.

Dudha Pokhari = Name of pond (sanctuary) which water look
likes the milk.

Manasolu = Name of a Himalayan Peak of Nepal,

Tarachok, Syage, Chipla = Names of villages

Sidhartha = Birth name of Buddha

Begnas, Rupa, Khaste, Dipang, Gunde, Neureni, and Maidee =
name of the lakes in Pokhara valley.

Adhikari = a Cast or a sub family name of Bramhan in Nepal.

Rastra Bank = Government bank of Nepal. Rastra means nation
in Nepali.

8: Bibliography:

Boo, Elizabeth. 1991. Ecotourism: The potentials and pitfalls. Volume 1, World wildlife
    Fund with the support of US agencies of International Development.

Borg, Jan Van Der. 1991. Tourism and Urban Development. The impacts of tourism on
    Urban development, towards a theory of urban tourism, and an application to the
    Case of Vanice, Italy.

Carrington, Patricia. 2002, International Ecotourism Society calls for improved
    Ecotourism Policy worldwide. News and Features from the International
    Ecotourism Society (IES). Alaska.

Cooper, Chris and Stephen Wan hill (Eds). 1997. Tourism Development Environment
    and
        Community issues. John Willey and Sons Chichesler. Newyork, Singapore, and
        Toronto.

ECOMOST Project. 1994. Planning for Sustainable Tourism. Published by International
    Federation of Tour Operators (IFTO), 170 High Street, East Sussex, UK.

Gurung, Horka. 1980. Vignettes of Nepal. Shaja Prakashan (Publisher), Katmandu.

Gurung, Horka. 1990. Environmental management of mountain tourism in Nepal.
        Published by International trade and tourism division of economic and social
        Commission for Asia and pacific region, Bangkok.

Hens luc and Nicholova (Eds). 2001. Tourism and Environment. VUB.

Honey, Martha. 1999. Ecotourism and sustainable development: who own Paradise?
    Publisher: Island press, Washington, DC, Covelo, CA.

Hunter, Colin and Haward Green. 1995. Tourism and Environment. London and
    Newyork.

ICIMOD's News letter for sustainable development in the Hindu Kush Himalayas. 1991.
    Policy focus for mountain development.

International Centre of Integrated mountain tourism (ICIMOD). 1998. Mountain tourism
    For community development in Nepal: A case study of Phewa lakeside, Pokhara,
    Nepal.

KC, Tilak.2000. Migration and its' consequences on tourism. Janapragyamanch
    Research Journal. Janapriya M. Campus Pokhara, Nepal. Year.1, No.1. Pp153-162.

Khatiwada, S. K.1998.Employment structure of tourism: A case study of Hotel Industries
    In Pokhara.

Lidde, Michael. 1997. Recreation Ecology. The Ecological Impact of out door, recreation
    and ecotourism, UK.

National Conservation Implementation Project (NCSIP), a report. 1997. Phewa Lake
    Conservation Action Plan: collaboration between the National Planning
    Commission and IUCN the world conservation, edited by Krishna P Oli. Pp 11-
23.

OECD. 1996. Tourism Policy and International tourism in OECED countries 1993-1994.
    Published by POLITIQUE DU TOURISME International...

Pradhan, M. G. 2001. Sustainable Tourism: Reality or rhetoric, a case study of
    Annapurna Conservation Area. University of Cambridge, Department of
    Geography. Pp-11.

Rastra Bank's research report. 2001. Problems, Challenges and achievement of Tourism Industry in Pokhara. 2001. Banking Development and Research Unit, Rastra Bank, Pokhara. Pp 3-75.

Research Methods and Evaluation book and journals. 20 years of publishing in South Asia. Sage publications, New Delhi, thousand oaks London.

Robinson, D. W. 1997. Strategies for alternative tourism: A case study of Tourism in Sagarmatha (Everest) national park of Nepal. In the Earth scan reader in the sustainable tourism, edited by Lesley France. Re-printed 1991.

Shrestha, Hiranya Lal. 1980. Naya Nepal Parichaya, 2039 B. A history of Nepal, published by M.K. Publisher, Katmandu.

Souvenir. 2000. Garden city of seven Lakes. Published by Lekhanath Municipality, Kaski, Nepal.

TAAN News letter. Sept 23, 2001. Trekking agent association o f Nepal. Vol. 2, No 2.

The Ecotourism Society.1998. Ecotourism: A guide for planners and managers vol 2. Published by Ecotourism Society North Bennington, Vermont. Edited by Lind berg, kreg, Megan Epler wood and David Engeldrum.

Tourism Policy 2052. 1995. His Majesty's Government, and Civil Aviation, Department of tourism Brikuti Mandap, Katmandu.

WTTC, WTO, and Earth Council.1996. Agenda 21 for the travel and Tourism industry: Towards Environmentally Sustainable Development. London,

http://www.nepalhomepage.com/travel/places/hilly/pokhara.html

http://www.lonelyplanet.com/maps/asia/nepal/

http://www.go2kathmandu.com/concerto/map.htm

Lightning Source UK Ltd.
Milton Keynes UK
UKOW051909250712

196566UK00001B/84/P